The Sun and Renewable Energy

Kaitlyn Duling

Cavendish
Square

New York

Published in 2020 by Cavendish Square Publishing, LLC
243 5th Avenue, Suite 136, New York, NY 10016

Library of Congress Cataloging-in-Publication Data

Names: Duling, Kaitlyn, author.
Title: The sun and renewable energy / Kaitlyn Duling.
Description: First edition. | New York : Cavendish Square, 2020. |
Series: The power of the Sun | Audience: Grades 2 to 5. | Includes bibliographical references and index.
Identifiers: LCCN 2018047155 (print) | LCCN 2018048581 (ebook) |
ISBN 9781502646811 (ebook) | ISBN 9781502646804 (library bound) |
ISBN 9781502646781 (pbk.) | ISBN 9781502646798 (6 pack)
Subjects: LCSH: Solar energy--Juvenile literature. |
Renewable energy sources--Juvenile literature. | Sun--Juvenile literature.
Classification: LCC TJ810.3 (ebook) | LCC TJ810.3 .D85 2020 (print) |
DDC 333.79/4--dc23
LC record available at https://lccn.loc.gov/2018047155

Editorial Director: David McNamara
Editor: Jodyanne Benson
Copy Editor: Nathan Heidelberger
Associate Art Director: Alan Sliwinski
Designer: Jessica Nevins
Production Coordinator: Karol Szymczuk
Photo Research: J8 Media

The photographs in this book are used by permission and through the courtesy of: Kessudap/Shutterstock.com; p. 1 (and used throughout) Black Prometheus/Shutterstock.com; p. 4 HektoR/Shutterstock.com; p. 7 (and used throughout) St-n1ce/Shutterstock.com: p. 8 Ssuaphotos/Shutterstock.com; p. 10 Pedrosala/Shutterstock.com; p. 12 Andrea Crisante/Shutterstock.com; p. 13 ArchOnez/Shutterstock.com; p. 14 Tom Grundy/Shutterstock.com; p. 16 Rsooll/Shutterstock.com; p. 18 Alf Ribeiro/Shutterstock.com; p. 19 Franco Lucato/Shutterstock.com; p. 20 Super Joseph/Shutterstock.com; p. 21 Brgfx/Shutterstock.com; p. 22 Gutzemberg/Shutterstock.com; p. 24 Robert Paul van Beets/Shutterstock.com; p. 26 Corlaffra/Shutterstock.com; p. 27 Martin33/Shutterstock.com.

Printed in the United States of America

Contents

The sun provides light, but its energy gives us so much more.

Chapter 1

The Sun's Energy

THE sun is a powerful star. It can give you a sunburn. It can also reduce your ice cream cone to a puddle. It lights our days and warms the oceans. Did you know that we also use its energy each and every day?

Fossil Fuels

When the sun shines, its energy is taken in by plants. The plants use it to create food that helps them to grow. The sun's energy gives us

SUN POWER
California has the highest number of houses powered by solar energy in the United States.

fruits and vegetables to eat. It also creates the beautiful, green world around us. All of that energy stays inside plants, even long after they have died. In fact, the energy can stay there for *millions* of years! Over time, plants are buried deep within the layers of Earth. They get pressed tightly together. They can turn into coal, oil, or natural gas. Because they are made from the remains of old plants and animals, we call these substances "fossil fuels." When we burn them, we can use that ancient energy.

Energy Sources

We are beginning to run out of these ancient energy sources. The supply of fossil fuels won't last forever. That's why they are known as **nonrenewable energy**. Luckily, there are

The Solar Calendar

Calendars are used to make sense of time and dates. Lunar calendars use the moon. Solar calendars use the sun. The one we use across the world today is a solar calendar. It is based on the seasons, which make up a full year of 365¼ days. This is how long it takes Earth to travel once around the sun. The first people to use a solar calendar were the ancient Egyptians.

renewable sources too. We can harness energy from wind, water, and the sun. These types of energy won't run out. They are known as **renewable energy**. We can draw from these sources again and again.

SUN POWER
The world has enough coal to last about 150 more years.

The size of a turbine and the wind's speed determine how much energy is produced from wind each day.

Chapter 2

Renewable Energy

THE sun offers many options for putting its energy to work in new and exciting ways. Renewable energy is power that can be made again and again. It never runs out.

Solar Energy

There are a few main types of renewable energy that the sun can help produce. The first type is solar energy. We get this energy from **solar cells**. A solar cell or solar panel is

A large-scale solar farm can cover hundreds of acres.

a piece of technology that changes light energy from the sun directly into electricity. You can see solar cells on houses, cars, and even streetlights. The first practical solar cell was invented in 1954. They have only just begun to gain in popularity. Lowering the price has helped. More and more people want to stop using nonrenewable energy. They are interested in switching to solar energy to heat their homes and provide their electricity.

Wind and Biofuel

Another surprising source of renewable energy is the wind. We can harness the power of the wind to generate electricity. We do this by installing large wind turbines with massive blades. When the blades spin through the air, a generator inside the turbine creates electricity. How cool is that? It doesn't release any pollution. The wind also never runs out.

How is the sun involved? Wind is caused by the uneven heating of Earth. Depending on the time of day and what the sun is shining on, the sun's light is absorbed differently by various parts of Earth, such as the ocean and

SUN POWER

Solar panels can be expensive. However, they can also lower your electric bill.

Wind turbines may look simple, but their interiors are full of technology.

the land. That uneven heating creates pressure changes in the atmosphere. When air moves between high-pressure and low-pressure areas, wind is created!

SUN POWER
There are over fifty-five thousand wind turbines in the United States.

We can also use renewable energy to power our vehicles. Gasoline is made of fossil fuels. **Biofuel** is made from living matter, like corn and soybeans. Crops and plants need the sun in order to grow. Today, one of the most popular types of biofuel is called **ethanol**. Ethanol is produced from corn and sometimes sugarcane. Biofuels burn more cleanly than fossil fuels. This means they create less pollution in the air. Renewable energy

Solar Energy on Cloudy Days

Do renewable energy sources work when the sun isn't shining? Yes! Say a family installs solar panels on their roof. On clear, sunny days, the panels may produce more energy than the family needs. This is stored for use on cloudy days, when less is produced. However, the sun is always sending energy to Earth, even if the clouds are out. You know this if you've ever gotten a sunburn on a cloudy day at the pool!

The same can be said of wind power. On blustery days, turbines store all the extra energy that isn't used immediately. That way, on calm days, there is still enough energy to power homes, schools, and businesses. Biofuels also work on cloudy and windy days if we grow the right ingredients.

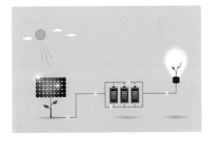

With a little help from solar panels, sunlight can provide the energy needed for a lightbulb.

can provide alternative power to cars, planes, boats, and other vehicles.

Getting Energy from the Sun

The amount of energy produced through wind turbines and solar panels all depends on how

Crops like soybeans need sunny days in order to grow well.

much the sun is shining and where it is shining. It also depends on whether we have installed the proper tools to harness that energy. We need to grow the right plants to make biofuels, too.

 ACTIVITY : Make a Solar Oven

You can harness the sun's energy to heat and cook food. All you need is a pizza box, aluminum foil, black paper, and plastic wrap. With a parent's help, cut a flap in the top of the pizza box, leaving it connected on one side. Wrap the entire flap in aluminum foil. Line the inside of the box with foil. Place a black sheet of paper inside the box. After placing it on a plate, put the food you want to cook on the black sheet of paper. You could melt a s'more or toast a piece of bread. Then cover the opening tightly in plastic wrap. Leave the oven in direct sunlight for a few hours. Voila! You have a tasty treat.

Corn needs sunlight, but too much heat can cause it to wither, or dry out.

Chapter 3

Seasons and the Sun

WHEN it comes to solar power and wind power, it is easy to see how much energy is being generated. Sunny days and windy days are the best. Cloudy, calm days are less helpful. However, these aren't the only types of renewable energy sources that the sun can provide. The sun is a big, powerful star! Scientists have discovered all sorts of ways to take advantage of its nearly endless supply of light and heat, no matter the season.

Some plants, like sugarcane, can be used to produce energy in cars.

Renewable Energy Sources Need the Sun

What's the one thing all renewable energy sources have in common? They are harnessing the power of the sun! Biofuels, for example, wouldn't work without the sun first shining down and putting its energy into the corn, sugarcane, and other plants that go into producing the fuels. That solar energy makes biofuels possible. We can only make biofuels if farmers have strong seasons and grow lots of corn and other plants.

The solar panel industry continues to grow and evolve with new technology.

Similarly, we can only make wind power if the wind is blowing. Solar panels work best when the sun is shining.

Engineers work hard to take advantage of solar energy in all seasons. For example, in the northern half of the globe, solar panels are built facing south. This helps them soak up the largest amount of sunshine. They work when the sun is shining but not

SUN POWER
Solar power is one of the cleanest renewable resources in the world.

producing too much heat. Wind turbines are built in windy places, like Texas.

Hydroelectric Power

Another form of renewable energy that you may not notice is **hydroelectric power**. In fact, hydroelectric power is one of the most common forms of renewable energy! This power is turned into electricity when water

Dams harness the energy of moving water to produce electricity.

flows through huge turbines on its
way to the sea. The turbines use
the energy to make electricity.
However, water doesn't have its
own power. Hydroelectric gets
its power from the sun! Heat energy drives
the **water cycle**. The sun heats water on
the oceans, and the water evaporates, or
changes from liquid to vapor. Later, the water

The ongoing water cycle affects Earth's weather patterns.

Solar Seasons

Is summer the best season for solar panels and wind turbines? Maybe not. Solar panels take in the light from the sun, not the heat. They actually work better in slightly cooler weather. In the United States, wind turbines perform best during the spring. Late summer is the worst time for wind power.

To some, wind turbines are beautiful additions to rural landscapes.

The Sun and Renewable Energy

vapor cools and turns back into liquid. This causes rain to fall. Some of the rainwater ends up in streams and rivers, which flow all the way to the ocean. Along the way, the motion of the water can become hydroelectric power. Did you know there were so many different ways to use the sun's energy to power our world? It really is incredible.

 ACTIVITY : The Power of Wind

How powerful can wind be? Let's find out! Hold a piece of string that is about 10 feet (3 meters) long. Have a friend or parent hold the other end, or tie it to a chair. Slip a plastic straw onto the string. Then, tape a balloon to the plastic straw. Blow up the balloon, holding the end shut. When you are ready, let go of the balloon. See how far the straw will move down the string! Next, try putting more or less air into the balloon. The energy needed to move the straw is created by the "wind" or air inside the balloon as it pushes out.

Some states are trying out multiple types of alternative energy sources.

Chapter 4

Solar Opportunities

AROUND the world, the potential for renewable energy continues to grow. It is becoming more affordable and more accepted by city planners and leaders. Some farmers even find themselves making more money using their land for wind farms than planting crops! Wind power, solar power, hydroelectric power, and biofuels all produce power by harnessing the same thing: the sun.

The sun is an incredible, unlimited, and clean source of energy. Every single day, it is shining on some part of our world.

Clean Energy

One of the best parts about solar energy is that it is renewable. It never runs out. We don't have to worry about losing it.

Solar panels on houses like this one in the Netherlands can provide hot water, electricity, and more.

 The Sun and Renewable Energy

Traditional power plants often emit dangerous pollution.

Using solar energy, whether in the form of wind, water, biofuels, or solar panels, is extremely clean. It doesn't produce the pollution that fossil fuels do. Right now, we are not taking full advantage of the resource that is our sun.

SUN POWER
China has the most solar panels in the world, followed by the United States.

Clean, limitless energy is available to us if we choose to make changes. We could burn less coal and build more turbines. We could also drill for less oil and make more biofuels. It's up to the next generations to transition as much as possible from nonrenewable energy to clean renewables. Our planet and our future depend on it!

Renewable energy keeps our planet clean and healthy so that it can be enjoyed by future generations.

Glossary

biofuel A type of fuel made from plants or other living things.

ethanol A kind of biofuel that is usually made from corn.

hydroelectric power Electricity that is generated when the movement of water turns large turbines.

nonrenewable energy Sources of energy that will one day run out.

renewable energy Limitless energy that will not run out.

solar cell A device that turns light energy into electricity.

water cycle The continuous process of water moving between Earth's surface, its atmosphere, and bodies of water.

Find Out More

Books

DeCristofano, Carolyn Cinami. *Running on Sunshine: How Does Solar Energy Work?* New York: HarperCollins, 2018.

Scibilia, Jade Zora. *Solar Panels: Harnessing the Power of the Sun*. New York: PowerKids Press, 2018.

Websites

NASA Climate Kids: Renewable Energy

https://climatekids.nasa.gov/menu/renewable-energy

Learn about the relationship between renewable energy and Earth's changing climate.

National Geographic: Biofuels

https://www.nationalgeographic.com/environment/global-warming/biofuel

Here, the National Geographic website outlines what biofuels are and how they work.

Index

Page numbers in **boldface** refer to images. Entries in **boldface** are glossary terms.

About the Author

Kaitlyn Duling believes in the power of words to change hearts, minds, and actions. An avid reader and writer who grew up in Illinois, she now resides in Washington, DC. She knows that knowledge of the past is the key to our future and wants to ensure that all children and families have access to high-quality information. Duling has written over fifty books for children and teens. You can learn more about her at http://www.kaitlynduling.com.